56 SECONDS

by

Sylvio (Syd) A. Gravel, MOM

Budd Publishing/Syd A. Gravel

Ottawa, Ontario

Copyright by Sylvio (Syd) A. Gravel, M.O.M., 2012
Published by: Budd Publishing/Syd A. Gravel

URL: http://www.56secondsbook.com

Library and Archives Canada Cataloguing in Publication

Gravel, Sylvio A., 1952-
    56 seconds / by Sylvio (Syd) A. Gravel.

Issued also in electronic format.
ISBN 978-0-9881316-0-6

    1. Post-traumatic stress disorder. 2. Police--Job stress.
3. Police psychology. 4. Gravel, Sylvio A., 1952-. I. Title.

RC552.P67G73 2012   616.85'21   C2012-905851-3

Print: ISBN 978-0-9881316-0-6
eBook: ISBN 978-0-9881316-1-3

Cover photographs courtesy of Clint Eastop
Cover illustration: www. istockphoto.com
Cover and Book Design: Budd Publishing
Editor: Eleanor Sawyer

PRINTED IN U.S.

To my loving wife and best friend

and

to those suffering alone and silent,

be alone and silent no more

Contents

Acknowledgements vii

Introduction 1

My Story 3

Moving Forward 11

    Posttraumatic Stress Disorder (PTSD) and Its Symptoms 14

    On Being a Hero 25

    Impact on the Family 26

The Spouse's Perspective 29

Letting Go 39

Twenty-Five Years Later 41

Peer Support History in Ottawa 43

    The Four Rules 45

    The Five Stages 45

    The Eight Most Common Symptoms 46

    Peer Supporters 47

    My Personal Involvement 48

After Word 51

Appendix 1: Three-Day Workshop: Introduction to Peer Support 53

Appendix 2: Two-Day Workshop for a Newly Established Peer
    Support Network 61

Appendix 3: Peer Support Meeting Where a Network Exists 67

About the Author 71

Acknowledgements

I would like to acknowledge several people who have contributed to this book in some way. First, I would like to thank J.J. Brun for being my coach and mentor, as well as my friend. I would also like to thank the members of the 2012 CAPS Fast Track Team for supporting each other in our first endeavours as speakers and authors.

Second, I would like to thank Dr. Pierre Turgeon, who first introduced the original members of the Robin's Blue Circle to each other. I also want to thank all the officers who have crossed paths with me over the years and shared their stories of pain and silent suffering. Maybe this book will allow you to step out of the darkness and be recognized as the victims and heroes that you are.

I want to thank Evelyn Budd of Budd Publishing for guiding me through the world of publishing and Eleanor Sawyer, my editor, for her input and feedback.

I also want to express my appreciation and love to my wife and my sons, who had no idea what they were going to have to live with by allowing me the dream of becoming a police officer.

And, finally, I want to thank the many who have gone before me, living in a world that they kept to themselves to the end of their lives.

May we all one day acknowledge their pain and the ultimate price they have paid to serve us.

Introduction

It had only taken fifty-six seconds to go through the entire incident from the moment I received a description of the armed robbery suspects to the moment when I called for an ambulance because I had shot a man.

After those brief fifty-six seconds, I was no longer the man who had first joined the police service. I now had a different perspective, based on hard-earned experience that I never had before. I became a changed man and I lost who I had once been.

I had hit a solid wall that I could not go through or pretend did not exist. Although I tried to circle back to find my original path in life, I couldn't. I now needed to learn how to continue my journey through life differently than how I had started. I now had the added weight of those fifty-six seconds of experience and memories as part of who I had now become.

Not everyone who is involved in a fatal or near-fatal incident suffers from posttraumatic stress disorder. I have spoken to many officers, who have had to shoot a suspect, and some were able to walk away unscathed, knowing that they had done the job expected of them. For there to be a trauma, there has to be a shock factor of some sort. There has to be an unexpected component that jars the involved person out of their ability to control their view of life.

For me, it was making a decision to react a certain way, based on a mix of a split-second accumulation of facts and assumptions. The end resulted in a man dying. His death was based on assumptions I made from his actions during the incident.

However, what he appeared to be doing at the time was not, in fact, what I had interpreted his actions to be. As a result, I experienced shock and post-shooting trauma.

It has taken me twenty-five years to share my story and this has not been easy to do. I have written this to help others understand the healing process and the steps I took, which have helped me to survive and which are now part of who I am.

This is my story of how it happened to me and how it can happen to you.

My Story

"No member of a police force shall discharge a firearm in the performance of duty except where, on reasonable or probable grounds, he believes it necessary for the defence. . . of the life of another." (Ontario Police Act, Reg. 790, Section 9[1] [a])

On a hot predawn August day, I protected my partner's life by shooting a young man to death. From that moment on, post-shooting trauma started to set in and I began to experience the violent emotions that jarred me with blow after unexpected blow.

In responding to an armed robbery, my partner and I found ourselves following, and stopping, a vehicle with two suspects in it. We asked the dispatcher to confirm the robbery suspects' descriptions. When we received the information over the radio, the two suspects in the car also heard the description given by the dispatcher and they took off, knowing that we had recognized them. My partner and I found ourselves in a high-speed chase.

After the suspects rammed into three parked cars, they were finally forced to stop and one of them abandoned their vehicle. A very short foot pursuit ensued. During this short time, several very clear and precise commands were given both by myself and my partner to the suspects to show their hands where they could be seen. I was very worried about the fact that I had not yet established which one of the suspects had a gun, or if they each had a gun, since we had been advised that we were responding to a 10-42. (Note: the 10-42 code refers to a robbery and a robbery always involves the use of force or a weapon. In this situation, the weapon used was not described, so for safety, a police officer assumes and reacts to the worst-case scenario, that is, that a gun had been used.) [1]

When the suspect I was primarily focused on stopped and turned to his left to look at me, after jumping on top of a parked car that was in his way, he had his right hand stuffed into the front of his jeans. I yelled at him several times to show me his hands as we locked eyes. But then he started to turn in the opposite direction toward my partner, who was standing off to the suspect's right side and focused on the other suspect.

As I had still not yet determined where the weapon was, I couldn't let him complete that turn. Because of the assumption that I had made that a gun had been used in the robbery, I couldn't give the suspect the opportunity to pull out a gun that he may have stuffed down the front of his pants. I drew up from the defensive stance and pointed my gun at the suspect and shot at him to stop him from continuing to turn toward my partner. It was the only way I could stop him from completing a dangerous motion toward my partner. I completed these actions from a distance of about thirty feet.

I was prepared to tap off two shots, as I had been trained, but the suspect went down as soon as I fired off the first shot. (Tapping off two shots—or pulling the trigger twice—was the standard shooting technique we were trained to use at that time.) As it turned out, and unbeknownst to me, the firing pin on my gun had broken after the first shot I took. I would not have been able to fire a second shot even if I had to. I first heard about the firing pin breaking, after that first shot, at the inquest held six months later.

I heard someone screaming to my right. Then, the suspect I had just shot stood up again and I got ready to fire off another shot if needed. However, it wasn't necessary, as he just stood straight up, then went down again.

I remember seeing a cloud of smoke spewing out of the barrel of my gun after the shot; the smoke seemed to hang in the air forever. The noise of the shot seemed to reverberate on and on. In the distance, I heard someone yelling, "I give up! I give up! Don't shoot. Don't shoot." The voice slowly got louder and louder. I suddenly realized that the other suspect was giving up, with his hands high up over his head. He was just a few feet to my right and still seated in the suspect's car.

At this point, other officers had started to arrive at the scene and I ran over to where the suspect I had shot laid on the ground. My partner was there already. The suspect was face down, rolling from side to side, then, after a few seconds, he finally stopped and just laid there. I called for an ambulance to get here as quickly as possible. We turned him over and pulled his hand out from the inside front of his pants. He had nothing in his right hand. There was no gun in his hand or on his person.

I fell back against the car. I started to sweat profusely. I had trouble breathing. I couldn't focus my eyes and the world started to spin. I felt nauseous as I realized that I had just shot an unarmed man. What had I done? I kept repeating the question over and over again to myself. From there, I went into shock—cold and hot flashes, sounds coming and going, sirens sounding so loud, then not hearing them at all, red lights flashing, trouble breathing, feeling nauseous, weak and trembling. People were talking to me but no sound was coming out of their mouths. Someone was touching my arm and I jumped off the ground as if I had been stabbed.

After some time, which seemed like a lifetime to me, the zone sergeant had the scene secured and the ambulance attendants removed the suspect from the scene. I vaguely remember being advised by someone in uniform that this was now a criminal investigation and I was a suspect. I was cautioned, given my rights and my gun was seized as evidence. I was then escorted away from the scene by a fellow officer and driven to the station.

From there, things were simply a real mixed bag of memories about what was going on around me. The investigators began their work and others seemed to be running everywhere all around me getting their work done.

My wife was contacted by members of the police association and a lawyer attended at the station to speak with me about my rights, since I was now subject to an investigation of a criminal nature. About an hour into the investigation, I recall the inspector on duty advising me that he had just received a phone call from the officer attending at the hospital; the suspect I had shot was pronounced dead. My legs gave out, I sat down and cried.

Nineteen hours after I had left home for work, and fourteen hours after the shooting, I returned home. By this time, I was exhausted and hungry. Every physical movement was difficult and required considerable effort. I tried to sleep but every time I started to fall asleep I would stop breathing. After being up for almost twenty-six hours, I was finally able to sleep fitfully for about four hours.

Later that morning, I received a number of phone calls from friends and fellow officers, who wanted to express their support for me at this time. These calls helped to break the ice between my wife and me. Oftentimes, my job was too gruesome, or the people I dealt with of such poor moral character, and I would not talk about what had happened during my workday. However, in this case, she needed to know what had happened in order to understand. By me talking on the phone with fellow officers, she was able to hear enough of my responses for me to talk to her. I was worried that I would scare, shock or confuse her with what had happened.

I knew I had done the only thing I could have done, as required of me as a police officer. But one moment I would feel relieved that I had done what was expected of me and the next moment I wondered what would have happened if I had hesitated one moment longer. Would the suspect be alive today? What if he had had a gun, as I first thought? Would he have shot my partner? How would I have been able to face my fellow officers if my partner had been hurt because I had hesitated one second too long? I despaired some more because no matter what, in this case, it appeared to me to be a no win decision. And now it became a matter of waiting to see if the police force also agreed with my actions.

At 10:00 AM the following morning, our local television station announced that the police administration was going to hold a press conference at noon to discuss the shooting the night before. My wife and I watched to hear the police state that they believed that I had followed proper procedures in this situation. Nobody had called me to advise me about what they were going to say. (I suppose they didn't have to but, as I did work for them, I would have appreciated it.)

Almost immediately, I started to develop some terrible mood swings. I became angry and disappointed that I had to watch television to find out what management thought about my actions rather than them telling me first; angry at a justice system that had allowed the suspect out of a federal penitentiary on mandatory supervision—without supervision; angry that I was the officer who had had to make the decision that cost him his life; and, finally, angry, then sad and frustrated, and then angry again! I was confused and now on an emotional rollercoaster that became more intense with every passing moment.

I was also suffering from intense and acute physical symptoms such as shortness of breath, chest pain, heavy perspiration and panic attacks. I was unable to find comfort in either sitting still or walking about.

Over the next few days, I read the newspaper reports and heard the newscasts and remained silent through it all, as required. I wanted to contact the suspect's family to offer my sincerest sympathies for the loss of their son, brother and husband. It wasn't their fault that the suspect had behaved as he did or that I had reacted the way I did. But the lawyers indicated that I should refrain from making any statement, so I refrained as advised. But I now began to question whether I wanted to go back to work, to wear the uniform or to keep the oath as a police officer.

Three days later, I did go back to work. The first night was the hardest. But it was better than staying at home and rethinking the incident over and over again. My first call on my first night back was a call to the south end of the city, where a warehouse alarm had gone off. I was the first officer on scene and was working alone. I went to the back of the warehouse and the back door was open. As I approached the door, the railroad tracks, which ran along the back of the warehouse, cracked in the heat and let out a loud bang—like a shot. I dropped to my stomach, gun in hand, wondering where the shot had come from. Within seconds, I was drenched in perspiration. Then, I realized what had happened and also how uptight I was.

Other officers arrived on scene and we checked the warehouse and found nothing. I went back to my cruiser and found the largest parking lot I could and sat there, right in the middle of the lot until the sun came up. Just sitting there in my police cruiser seemed like a pointless way to put in the rest of the shift. But at least I was back and I had put in my first shift.

It had only taken fifty-six seconds to go through that entire incident from the moment I received a description of the suspects to the moment I called for an ambulance—fifty-six seconds to destroy four cars, one front-yard fence, two front lawns within a distance of almost a kilometre. Fifty-six seconds and one man was dead and my entire outlook on policing had changed drastically.

But the most difficult stages were yet to come. I believed in my ability to make the right decisions but this had now been shaken. I believed in the training that I had received and in the things that I had been taught. But I began to question whether I could do what was required of me if I had to.

As I had been trained, I saw how fast I could react without thinking. But I worried that, because of what had happened, would I hesitate now? Would I take a second too long to think about it? Would I be able to react fast enough? And now that I had seen how fast I could react, would thinking about what had happened, and how fast it can happen, make me a liability now?

Although I came to appreciate all those who supported my wife and me through those trying times, I also needed to know that I had the support of the community, which I had sworn to protect. If this support was taken away from me, then there was no purpose in policing this community. No officer, who has sworn to devote their life to the safety of their community, should feel the scorn of their community after being forced to do something no one else would have wanted, or be prepared, to do.

After several weeks of feeling very lonely, I met with several other officers who approached me, one at a time, to tell me that they understood how I felt. I found out that these officers had also been involved in shootings. Soon, we all met for the first time to discuss how to help each other through these trying times. We became known as a peer support network for officers involved in death or near-death events directly related to the responsibilities of police work; we took the name Robin's Blue Circle. It wasn't long before we were being called by other officers, who also were going through trauma. Before long, we were recognized locally as a credible group to call in after-shooting incidents within our area.

Endnote

1. The inquest into this shooting changed code 10 to require the revelation of the weapon used such as 10-42 with a knife, 10-42 with a gun, 10-42 no weapon seen, so that officers did not have to assume the worst but could work with facts.

Moving Forward

It took six years for the courts to close the file on my shooting. This included the criminal investigation into both my actions and the actions of the robbery suspects; the inquest; the civil case; and the criminal proceedings against the second suspect, which worked their way through the courts.

I was absolutely convinced during those six years that I had no control over my own life, that all these individuals involved in the justice system surrounding my case were the only ones who could, and would, decide what I would do, how I would think and how I would live.

What also didn't help during this time was dealing with workers' compensation. It took two appeals before my claim for an illness, directly related to this incident, was approved. Once approved, I was advised by the final arbitrator for the compensation board that my claim should never have been denied to begin with. This frustrating process didn't help the healing and it is little wonder now that officers hire lawyers to represent their interests in the claims process.

For six years, I kept a solid professional demeanour, although I would hardly speak to anyone. I intentionally became a social recluse and, on the day that the judge closed the file after the final process in the civil case, I collapsed. Suddenly, six years after the event, when everything reached its conclusion, I found myself breaking down emotionally and was physically exhausted. My wife, close friends, members of my peer support network and my family doctor stepped in to help.

The doctor placed me under his care for two months. During this time, I slept almost continuously—was overcome with despair frequently—and was very angry. I also spent considerable time mulling over the events again and again. I was developing an unhealthy state of mind.

But I also spoke a lot with my peer support network and my wife about how confused I felt. During this very difficult time, I developed close relationships within my peer support network and rediscovered my intense love for my family.

This period was a crucial time in my life and those relationships were absolutely necessary for me to survive the next stages in my life. Suddenly, six years after the event, I was now deep in the midst of suffering from the many symptoms of post-shooting trauma. Although I loved police work, I just didn't know if I wanted to continue to be a part of a work world that included causing a death and all the processes involved as a result. Eventually, through the strong support of my family and friends, I returned to work.

What helped me to recover quickly was the normalcy of the workplace. I truly believe that the faster one gets back to work, the more normal life becomes. When I arrived at the station and went to the locker room to change into my uniform, everyone else was doing the same thing and chatting away about life in general as they always did. Nobody took issue with the fact that I had been away for awhile or why. I was welcomed back by everyone by no one making a big deal about my return to work. It was almost as though I had not left and that my presence at work was normal. And it was the right thing for them to do.

Even though I was already a rather tough-skinned individual from my upbringing and from some experiences I had encountered in dealing with difficult situations in my career prior to the 1987 shooting incident, I still had a very difficult time coping.

As a young man just out of college, I worked for a private company in Tanzania. In 1972, I was assigned to survey along the border between Tanzania and Mozambique. At the time, Mozambique was in the midst of the Frelimo Revolution. Unfortunately, for me, I was in the wrong place at the wrong time. Late one evening, I found myself surrounded by Tanzanian soldiers and I was detained. I was suspected of being a mercenary against the Frelimo and hiding on the Tanzanian side of the border. I spent almost a month recovering from that experience, which included being incarcerated as a prisoner for ten days. I came out of that experience tougher in character.

Then, years later, during my first week on the job as a police officer, along with my officer coach, I was involved in the vehicle pursuit of two armed suspects, who had robbed a cornerstore in a neighbouring community and had ended up in our city. At one point during the pursuit, I was standing in front of the suspect vehicle, when the suspect driving the getaway car tried to run me over. I jumped to the side of the road, rolled and then took a shot at the driver. I missed the driver, fortunately, but the glass shattered and eventually he lost control of the car. We caught both of them. But I was charged, convicted and fined three day's pay under the Ontario Provincial Police Act for the unlawful discharge of a firearm. It had been determined that, since I had dodged getting run over by jumping to the side of the road, then there was no longer a danger to my life. Firing a shot toward the driver was not a defendable action.

In both of these past experiences, I was at the receiving end of the consequences of being in a place or acting in a certain way. In the fifty-six seconds incident, someone else had suffered the consequences of my actions and had died. I found the aftermath of that hard to take. It didn't matter to me that the situation called for a certain action, validated by law or by accepted police practice, a life had been lost and it tore at my heart and my personal beliefs.

The taking of a life is contrary to everything that I believe in. I became a police officer because I strongly believed that I could do something to make our world a better place in which to live. This belief is not as naive as it may sound. Many may talk about making the world a better place but it is the police, firefighters, nurses and doctors and many others in the service industry who are actually involved in doing so.

Posttraumatic Stress Disorder (PTSD) and Its Symptoms

As a result of those fifty-six seconds in my life, for the past twenty-five years, I have suffered from the eight symptoms, which many recognize as fairly common to those who suffer PTSD. For those who have never been through it personally, it can be quite a shocking process to work through. With the help of my peer support network and family, I was able to deal with these symptoms.

1. Denial

One of the most commonly acknowledged symptoms is that of denial. Officers suffering from work-related trauma will, more often than not, deny that they even have a problem in dealing with a given situation, even though they may be showing signs of suffering. They will isolate themselves; lose control of their emotions and become impatient, angry and frustrated with those around them; abuse alcohol and become abusive in relationships; have thoughts of running away to be alone; and may even go so far as to consider or even attempt suicide. Yet they still deny that they are having a problem when someone reaches out to them. Admitting to the situation is the first step in healing oneself.

2. Loneliness

The feeling of loneliness is a very delicate issue to deal with for both the sufferer and members of a support group. This is not about isolation but rather about the feeling of aloneness where a person says in public, "There is no one there." "I felt deserted." "No one understands." When this is said, some people are offended and respond, "After all we've done for him or her." "How ungrateful can he or she be? " The problem is in being able to understand exactly what it is the person is saying. This person is calling out for help. This person is not saying that no one listened to them after a traumatic event occurred or that no one cared; they are asking, "Does anyone really know what I am going through?"

The speed with which an incident occurs leaves no time for a person to lean on another officer's experience or knowledge, so that a decision can be confirmed. Once a decision has been made, right or wrong, and no matter how many officers there are after the fact to offer their sympathy and understanding, only one officer stands alone, having made a final decision or taken the last step.

Only one officer will be questioned many times over about why they pulled the trigger or how or why an individual was shot, or why the officer did what they did. Only one officer takes the stand at the inquest and tells the family members what happened. Only one officer faces the scrutiny that follows from the media and the rumours that may circulate.

Only one person looks in the mirror every morning and rethinks the scenario over and over again, wondering—with all the questioning that they have gone through with the investigators, hearing all the comments from the public and reading the media's reports on what happened—did I or did I not do the right thing? Therein lies the loneliness and the sense of being alone that follows.

3. Second Guessing and Loss of Self-confidence

For me, the most difficult, most hard-hitting and the longest-lasting symptoms were those of second guessing my actions and responses during those fifty-six seconds and dealing with the resulting tremendous loss of self-confidence.

The individual who thought they were doing all the right things just doesn't know any more. They now find the decision-making process, even in their personal life, very difficult. But, no matter how intense the pressure gets, the officer must be supported in knowing that the right thing was done at the time; this must never be taken away from the officer.

I remember coming home one evening after a rather difficult and demanding day at work and my wife asking me if I would like chicken or beef for dinner. I exploded, demanding to know why I was the one who always had to make the decisions and yelling out that the last time I had to make a decision someone had died. "Why can't someone else decide everything from now on?" I yelled. It was way over the top but very much a part of the symptoms of posttraumatic stress. I was embarrassed and apologized for my outburst, but I realized that it was part of reliving the event.

Those who suffer from PTSD are forever second guessing every decision they make, simply because they now know that each and every decision can be twisted to mean something else and can have severe consequences. A sense of paranoia creeps into their life.

Where their security rests at work is in the training they have received, their will to survive and the strong support of their peers, family, community and superiors. This is why training is so important. And it is equally important to spend some time discussing training and how it relates to self-confidence and second guessing.

I was a professional development police instructor for many years in my career after my shooting incidents and, based on my experiences in observing officers who have made use-of-force decisions, no one can know how another person will react in every given situation. The necessity for the officer at the scene to address all the impact factors is absolutely that officer's decision and his or hers alone.

Real-life situations cannot be brought into a classroom. Nor can they be duplicated by anyone else at any other time, even at a scene. Nor can they be speculated on. Nor does a real-life situation compare to the classroom situations.

There is no doubt that the purpose of academic exercises is to accentuate the importance of various aspects of the law and how police officers are expected to work within them. These simulation exercises, sometimes using *simunition* (as we prefer to call training exercises or scenarios and the use of fake ammunition in police jargon), serve the purpose of demonstrating and articulating to the participants the legal parameters under which they are expected to work within the law. These simunitions help establish a knowledge and awareness baseline from which the officers can work.

These exercises are acted out in controlled, academic and sterile environments, devoid of all the unpredictable, emotional human intensity and interactions that officers will face on the streets. We use real-life situations that have been shared with us by our officers on the streets. But we rarely ever end up with the exact same end results that they did. However, using these real-life examples allows instructors to interject with comments and questions, and stop the action to make a point. It also allows participants to ask *what-if* questions in relation to how things should have, could have or would have been done.

For the most part, most instructors try to limit the number of what-if questions as much as possible, especially if more experienced officers are being instructed. The longer their personal experience, the more complex the number of what-if situations for discussion become, since they now know that no two situations are ever the same, even from one minute to the next. The best an instructor can hope for is that the officers come to understand how complex things can get on the street or in any given situation.

The simulations all boiled down to hoping that the following key points were passed on and retained by the officers:

- No matter what happens, we expect you to go home at the end of your shift.
- Know your authority and do not abuse it.
- Know your use-of-force continuum and do not abuse it.
- Know your equipment.
- Be prepared to articulate why you did what you did, because

you are the only one who can explain what you were thinking at the time, which led you to do what you did.

- Be prepared to be responsible for and live with the consequences of your decisions.

There are so many variables, which can be involved in every arrest, use of force or investigation simulation from one second to the other, that it's important to keep simunitions focused on an intended path to prove a point and not necessarily to address everything that officers will actually experience in real life. The idea is to share what could be the best or the worst outcome for them to learn from.

The simulations allow for discussions about what could be the best outcome from them. At best, officers will remember the simulation, when faced with real-life situations, and, at the very least, it will help them to measure their thoughts, actions and words from a baseline of knowledge that they gained from participating in these simulations.

Most professional police instructors know never to assume that, once these officers have participated in these simulations, they now know how to react in all real-life situations. No matter how close to the incident the simulation may appear, it always lacks the unpredictable and ever-changing impact factors of real life.

The decisions officers make on the streets—though founded on the best training that can be given in sterile academic settings, including participation in controlled simulations, using actors, and based on real-life incidents experienced by other officers— are theirs and theirs alone to make, articulate and be responsible for and live with. In real life, police officers have to take into account all the impact factors that present themselves in the situation and at a given moment.

The Ontario Police College used the real-life incident from my life as a training simulation for recruits. It was deemed to be a damned if you do, damned if you don't simulation. It challenged recruits to think about their actions and to articulate why they did what they did. There were any number of actions and responses. They could either shoot or not; either decision could be right or wrong, depending on what they saw, felt, smelled, heard, how they were brought up, what level of education they achieved, if they were able to quickly assess a life or death situation, think critically, what they had experienced in their personal life in the past, how they were taught to make decisions, how they learned to react under tense situations, what they thought was expected of them on this day in this simulation and knowing that their career depended on making a good impression at the college. The list of factors goes on and on.

I attended the college as a senior officer course participant one year after the shooting in which I was involved. I had an opportunity to discuss with an instructor how recruits acted out how they would react to my event, if it was them instead of me taking a decision. I was amazed and impressed with the wide range of descriptions, thoughts and feelings articulated by the recruits as they explained why some of them decided to shoot and others did not. The impact factors that affected their decision-making were theirs, and theirs alone, to decide from and to live with.

It helped me tremendously to see and hear other officers try to explain their way through my shooting incident. It helped me to understand why I was so confused. There really were so many ways in which the event could have played out, depending on so many factors.

4. Loss of Emotional Control

A roller-coaster ride of emotions usually occurs immediately after such an incident. And, for some officers, this can go on for years and have an extreme impact on their ability to live their lives. Part of the emotional rollercoaster can also include the officer's point of view about how he perceives his actions in relation to policing as an honourable profession.

For example, one officer committed suicide even as he was sharing, with other members of a peer support network, his difficulty in dealing with his situation. He was also under his family doctor's care at the time. It is important for officers to understand that flashbacks can and do occur.

Others may have difficulty controlling how they feel about an incident itself. One moment they are extremely proud of how well they have reacted to the life or death situation and may even express this feeling verbally. Then, suddenly, without warning, the tears will begin to flow and they will be overwhelmed with despair. For some, it becomes a matter of wondering when the next emotional attack will happen and what will trigger it (e.g., a sound, a sight or a smell).

Officers need to know that this emotional rollercoaster is a normal part of posttraumatic stress disorder and is one of the symptoms that his peer supporters will look for. Once the individual understands this reaction, then, they can accept it and move on.

5. Loss of Sleep and Appetite Control

Many officers noticed a loss of sleep for the next day or so after the incident, until exhaustion takes over. This is normal. The adrenaline rush alone, which the officer has just gone through, will be powerful enough to knock sleep out of their system for some time. Some officers have reported that they stopped breathing every time they fell asleep and weren't able to sleep until they were totally exhausted. They reported this lasted for several days and even came back without warning years later. (I suffered from this twenty-five years later as a result of writing this book and sharing my story.)

Some found themselves suddenly gaining uncontrolled amounts of weight; others have found that they weren't able to eat anything for days after the incident and lost weight. Officers should be advised to speak with their family doctor as soon as possible after an incident, if they suffer from any sort of gastric problem or eating disorder.

Officers should also avoid drinking coffee, tea and soft drinks for a few days and possibly restrict their liquid intake to fruit juices and water. Eating small snacks, as opposed to big meals, for a few days also helps. There should be absolutely no alcohol consumed for at least a few days, or even longer, and, for some, never again. And, no alcohol should be taken, when there is a loss of emotional control or a loss of sleep, due to reliving the incident.

Unless prescribed by your family doctor, police officers should stay away from all drugs. The indiscriminate use of drugs will tear apart your inner strength and your inner core, the family, your loved ones and your social circle. During this stressful time, you need to be able to control your already fragile state of mind and your emotions, as well as your decision-making process. Drugs will interfere with your ability to cope with the stress and trauma you are experiencing. The same holds true for alcohol when used indiscriminately without control.

Unlike so many who fall victim to alcohol abuse in our profession, I stayed away from it as a crutch. While walking the beat on the streets of Ottawa, I had met many highly decorated heroes (veterans from our armed forces), sleeping in cardboard boxes in the midst of winter, slowly killing themselves through alcohol abuse. I did not want to go there!

6. Obsessing over Public Perception

Under normal circumstances, police officers usually ignore public opinion that contradicts law enforcement; otherwise, they would have difficulty doing their work. However, when they are suffering from posttraumatic stress, they may find that their emotional stability is weakened and public opinion may affect them as it never has before. It may even seem to others that they are obsessing over what the public may think about their actions. Their peers, family and friends may not understand why they place any importance on the public's opinions now. Or they themselves may not understand why their peers, family and friends place any importance on public perception. But, nevertheless, it has an impact on everyone involved.

Of course, their life and their work will be affected, if they are under the impression that the public doesn't support them. Nevertheless, they need to be prepared for their new response to public opinion. Their will or ability to move on may be hampered by a need to respond to public perception.

An officer involved in a shooting incident must be prepared for the dangers of giving any value to any misguided or manipulated public agendas, to any sensationalized reporting in the media or value to any media commentators. After all, their job is to report what makes news and generate interesting discussions no matter the availability of the facts.

7. Fear of Loss of Peer Support

There are three areas where officers look for support. Professionally, they will look to their peers and to their superiors. Personally, they will look to their immediate family first, then to the extended family, for support. They will then look to the community.

Those going through the effects of post-shooting trauma should take advantage of every good wish extended to them. Their friends will want to help them as they go through their worst nightmare. Officers should be reminded to cherish those well wishes and not brush them off or deny that they are needed.

An officer may find it difficult to talk about the incident and, in fact, may not want to talk about it at all. However, it is important for the officer not to alienate their peers, family or friends. Although the support network may not understand why they won't talk, its members need to accept the officer's wishes. When the time comes, the officer will open up.

At some point, the officer is going to recover from these symptoms and his peers are going to be there to welcome him (or her) back and work with him. Paying attention to each other's feelings can help make things easier later.

8. Fear of Not Protecting Family and Loved Ones

Often an officer's loved ones will suffer as much as they do as they watch him/her go through the effects of a post-shooting trauma. Watching certain traumatic reactions may frighten family or concern them deeply. Officers need to be cautious about how they treat those around them. They may hurt their loved ones without even realizing it. This would be the worst time for this to happen. This is a time when they need to lean heavily on those who will support them the most.

Isolation can be a good thing. It gives an individual time to sort through thoughts and emotions. But isolation to the point where they are disconnected from their family, friends or peers is not good. Isolation is beneficial as long as it does not interfere with the lines of communication and any help being offered. Sharing with family members that an officer needs some time alone just to make some sense of how they feel is all right, as long as feelings are shared with the family later.

Police officers need to recognize that the desire or need to protect their family from the effects they are experiencing is a symptom of PTSD. (To learn how PTSD impacts the spouse, *see* the next chapter titled "A Spouse's Perspective.")

On Being a Hero

I once asked how two undercover officers could have been shot and wounded among a crowd of civilians on a street after a bank robbery. How could the robbers distinguish them from everyone else in the crowd? The suspects answered, "When everyone else was running away, they were the only two running towards us."

This responsibility to run toward danger, when everyone else is running away from it, is assumed by every officer when they decide to join the police force. I like to believe that all police officers are heroes for choosing to take on this responsibility. Police officers know that they are doing something that very few others are willing to do. But, in accepting this role as part of a police officer's duties, it carries with it some incredible pressures and high expectations that they will always do the right thing. They are equally aware that the community also has expectations that police officers will act correctly in fulfilling their job.

This role as police officers makes it difficult for us to exhibit human failings. We come to believe that we should show no fear, no hesitation to act or to be seen as unwilling to do what has to be done. For example, one officer committed suicide when he reached a point where he felt so strongly that he had shamed the police community by his actions.

He had placed policing on such a high pedestal of values that no one could have lived up to them. When he made what he incorrectly thought was a terrible decision that ran contrary to how police officers should behave, he despaired. In spite of all the peer, family and medical support, he took his life.

These pressures create an unhealthy and unrealistic environment for us to live in. And, sometimes, we fail in our duty. This is when we require time and help, so that we can return to our jobs and take up our duties and responsibilities to the community, including those of running toward danger, when all others are fleeing.

Impact on the Family

Police officers should remember that, when they are at home, they must be spouses first, not officers. Bringing home the uniform is rarely a good thing to do. Children already know their parent is a police officer; they need a parent. Spouses already know they are married to a police officer; they need a spouse and a friend. When dealing with difficult situations at home, being a family member first and foremost is best.

It is important to establish routines that support the ability not only of the officer to speak to their family members but also to learn to listen to them. As an example, one member shared with his peers how it was a routine in their home for his spouse and him to always do the dishes together after their meals. This gave them an opportunity to talk to each other without the children around (the children always left the kitchen in order to avoid doing the dishes anyway). Other officers shared that they always made it a point to stop whatever it was they were doing, regardless of how important it seemed to be at the time, to listen to their children.

If impatience, irritability or violence creep into an officer's behaviour at home, after an officer has faced a stressful or traumatic situation or incident at work and may be suffering from PTSD, then the officer should seek counselling from supportive peers, as well as medical support.

Creating good communication habits with members of the family right from the beginning will help when it becomes necessary to communicate in a stressful situation.

Officers also need to know that, at times, it may be difficult to share with their spouse what happened at work. For the most part, sharing most issues is not necessary. However, when things become so difficult that officers begin to avoid coming home to their family for fear of having to share their pain, this is the time when the officer most needs to go home.

The Spouse's Perspective

The following letter was written by a spouse whose husband also suffered from posttraumatic stress disorder (PTSD); she discusses the impact of the job and PTSD on her and the family.[1]

Dear Syd,

My husband can be a pretty funny guy. It was part of—well probably a big part of—what attracted me to him. His love of sports (because I don't have a competitive bone in my body) and the fact that he liked coaching kids' baseball impressed me. He was smart, fiercely loyal, proud and, unfortunately, stubborn like me. He had a wonderful family; I knew that because I was introduced to him through his sister whom I worked with.

We had a pretty short engagement by today's standards and married on his twenty-third birthday. It could be argued that, maybe, we didn't know enough about each other. But we knew we were in love and I knew that he was a good person and hard worker who would love and provide for his family. Those traits would soon be needed as we quickly had two daughters, and then he applied and was accepted into the RCMP. We moved to Alberta, away from our parents and siblings, and lived in four different places during our twenty-two years in the province.

I won't go through all the experiences he has had within the force. But I will say he has been very successful, and being an RCMP family has been an interesting challenge. When he went through training, he paid close attention when they told him not to tell the family too much about what was going on at work. We were spared the gory details about what actually went on in his shifts and how it affected him. Instead, he always tried to find something positive to tell us about the job that he loved. I would describe him as having a vibrant personality and someone who easily connected with others, a team player who possessed a "cup half-full" outlook on life.

When our children were ages sixteen, fourteen, three and one, he was one of a handful of RCMP members successful in being chosen to do a United Nations International Policing Tour in Sierra Leone, Africa. His mission was nine months/two tours in one of the worst postings. My biggest regret is that, within six months of him coming home, I realized he still wasn't "out of Africa" and I didn't tell a professional.

Our family life and marriage were nothing like before. What we were dealing with was his difficulty connecting due to posttraumatic stress disorder. We were basically living separate lives—me and the kids, he and the RCMP. Work provided his place of stability but, at the same time, the harder and longer he worked, the more distant he grew from us. Can you imagine living a life where the most stressful part of your day was coming home to your family? So, we just carried on living, working, existing within our marriage and raising kids who basically had forgotten how their dad used to be. Our bond as a couple was disintegrating. I ended up depressed and, despite all of this, we carried on like a "normal" family.

When the allegations of inappropriate professional and personal behaviour came to light, in my anger and in disbelief, I begged him to answer the question, "Who are you?" Despite our difficulties, I was shocked as the behaviour was so totally out of character, so totally against his values and moral fibre.

Alcohol has been used to debrief after a huge case or as part of the accepted celebration for a gruelling job well done within the RCMP. Most RCMP spouses would agree with this. Within their world, police deal with some incredibly horrific things. I couldn't do their job but I thank God that somebody does and we have police to protect us.

The expectation that police officers act in an exemplary manner is reasonable; however, the men and women working within the RCMP are human beings, not robots. Human beings with the same frailty as you and me, who are expected to put their lives on the line fearlessly day in day out. Expected to do this work with understanding, courage, strength, and empathy in the most volatile and devastating situations. Yet it's never supposed to be too much for them to handle.

Alcohol became my husband's way of handling things, numbing things, coping and avoiding his mental closet, where he stuffed the atrocities and suffering he has experienced throughout his career. Alcohol helped him avoid feeling and keep his closet doors shut. Africa seems to have been the straw that broke the camel's back and, after Sierra Leone, his closet grew to become a huge walk-in with bulging doors.

After hitting rock bottom, he started to change. Throughout the following three years, I've seen the man I love, and married over twenty-six years ago, work hard to become a better person. He admitted his mistakes and apologized, and never made excuses. He quit drinking, has been involved in ongoing therapy and, again, has become an emotionally involved, loving dad and husband. I have observed his commitment of continuing to go to work, and excel at times, within an environment nothing short of schoolyard bullying.

We transferred to our home province, which was a move decided by the RCMP. But we were optimistic and hoping for a fresh start. My husband was looking forward to beginning work at his new posting and showed me positive emails he had received from the office. From what was written, it appeared they were excited to have him on board.

Eventually, his past behaviour came back to haunt us and, days after the story broke in the media, a cameraperson and reporter were banging on the front door of our new home. Due to the extensive media coverage, we even had to divulge their dad's situation to our elementary school age children, which was understandably an incredibly painful discussion. The media has chosen to continue covering my husband's story like he's the poster boy for bad behaviour in the RCMP. And the force certainly seems to be making an example of him. I guess if you focus on one person long enough it diverts attention from everyone else.

I am interested to know though, why the media believes an RCMP officer with two criminal convictions for drunk driving deserves better treatment and anonymity? And, while we're at it, why are other employees, who were also involved with my husband at that time, avoiding the same scrutiny my husband has been subjected to?

My husband has used the saying, "No matter how thin you make a pancake, there are always two sides." It is a saying he uses when dealing with people during cases he is involved in, no matter how obvious things appear. Sometimes, it surprises you when you find out the other side. Maybe—maybe not—this information will show the other side.

I do hope that in reading this you will find it in your hearts to show me, my husband and our families some compassion. We all make mistakes because we are human. If you've never made a mistake, then carry on; otherwise, please grant us some peace.

Sincerely,
A Spouse

My spouse also shares her thoughts and perspective as it related to living with me through my post-shooting experience.

When the incident happened to my husband, he called me and said, "I just shot a person." I could hear him choking on the words and forcing himself not to cry. I called on some friends to take care of our two sons so that I could go to the station to be with Syd.

The first thing that came to mind for me was to protect him because I knew he would be hurting. I knew him well enough to know that, even though he had been trained to protect society, which might mean having to use lethal force if necessary, it is the most unnatural thing to shoot someone. He would have done everything in his power to avoid reaching this stage. I knew that this was very difficult for him.

I didn't realize it at the time but, in order to do what he had to, he had had to shift into another realm, because everything was so unreal to him. He had to rely on his training and then shift back to his previous self once the task was accomplished. But it was this shifting from one person to another that caused him to go into a state of shock. I didn't realize how much of a shock it would be to him and what the consequences would be for me and our family.

At the police station, two officers came to get me. They told me that Syd was all right and that they wanted to bring me into the station so that I could be there if he needed me. When I arrived, Syd gave me a hug. But I knew he was not with me; he was a bundle of nerves. However, he saw me and that calmed him down a bit. I could see it in his eyes.

He had a lot of paperwork to do and some people wanted to talk to him. He couldn't talk to me about anything other than to tell me he was okay, the suspect was shot and at the hospital. As I waited, I heard one of the senior officers tell him that the suspect was dead. Syd was absolutely devastated by the news.

While I was waiting for Syd, two patrol officers—one who did not know who I was—were talking back and forth about the shooting incident as they got ready to start their shifts. One officer asked the other, "Why would he shoot a guy just for a few bucks?" Then he asked, "If he didn't have a gun why did he shoot him?" The second officer told the first one to shut up as he recognized me as Syd's spouse. They left the room and I was left sitting there in the waiting room by myself, wondering why they would ask these questions without knowing what had happened to Syd. I was really becoming worried that my husband would not get any support.

Shortly after this, Syd suddenly showed up in the waiting room. He said we could go home. So we drove home and I remember being followed by a car with two officers in it. Once home, I simply paid attention to Syd. But he was not approachable. He wouldn't let me hug him or even talk to him. He simply sat there staring into space. I tried to normalize the environment by making some food and just keeping the house quiet.

But my husband was in another world. He wouldn't talk or even move. He just sat there as if in a trance. I was supposed to go to work the next day but I knew I had to stay home with Syd, so I called in to get time off. Although my employer gave the time to me, they were quite upset that I was taking time off on such short notice.

The following Monday morning, I called our family doctor to make an appointment for Syd to see him. I then called the police association for some help, because Syd was not coming out of the trance that he was in.

There were some announcements on TV about the shooting, so Syd and I sat together to watch the news. But he still wouldn't say anything.

Finally, we saw Syd's doctor that Monday. He and Syd chatted and his doctor thought that Syd would be fine, he just needed time. The police association called and told me to call a professor, who said he would help. I called him and he spoke with Syd and reassured him that everything he was going through was normal, that he just had to realize this and not worry about it.

On Tuesday, I returned to work and left Syd at home alone. He didn't like being at home alone—too much reliving of the incident—and, on Wednesday, he went back to work. I didn't think he was ready but he wanted "to get back in the saddle" as he put it.

I was also worried about our sons. They were young and the news about the shooting incident was widespread. I went to the school to talk to the principal. School staff agreed to keep an eye on the boys.

Syd and I both went to see the professor at the University of Ottawa. He explained to us what Syd would probably end up going through. We already recognized some of the symptoms and behaviours, such as the shortness of breath; the anxiety attacks, depression and mood swings; the loss of appetite and sleep; and the emotional rollercoaster of, first, being proud of having done what he had to do and, then, being angry and depressed for having done what he had to do. He was so confused!

It took some time for my husband to let me into his world. But, over time and with the help of the many phone calls he received, I was able to hear enough from those conversations to help him see that I too understood.

We started to go for long walks and just talk—or not. But we walked whether anything was said or not. He always felt better when we finished those walks, so I made a point of doing it with him every chance we had. We would concentrate on the sunsets and the sunrises and just sit together and watch them through long moments of silence.

Finally, over time, Syd started to share his feelings with me and, once he started, he never stopped. He let it all pour out and, from then on, he shared everything with me that bothered him about work or that he was proud of as a result of his work. There were no more secrets about what his work required of him.

He shared with me how scared he was about having to make another decision of the same kind. However, he also knew that he had a responsibility to his work and to his family. I tried to convince him to resign and go back to school to get his degree. But he wouldn't quit. He felt that this would be seen as a weakness and he kept struggling to go to work every day.

Eventually, he settled into his new world. When he had first started working with the police, he developed a large circle of friends and we socialized a lot. Now, he latched on to two or three people and they became the only people he was willing to talk to. Although he talked a lot, I noticed that his conversations with people were very superficial. He never entered into a conversation of any depth with any of them.

He was afraid of alcohol because he thought he couldn't control his emotions when he drank and also because of his experience walking the beat. He worked out in the gym every day and went from 160 to 250 pounds of solid muscle.

He had difficulty controlling his emotions, losing his temper quickly but recovering quickly as well. He would cry, without notice or for no apparent reason, with tears streaming down his cheeks. I learned not to say anything or ask him anything when these moments occurred. He needed to sort things out himself.

I had to remind him to pay attention to his sons. At first, he tried to stay away from them because he didn't want people associating them with him. Eventually, he came to realize how short a memory the public has. And Syd and his two sons developed a great relationship. The boys loved it when Dad made supper because I was working evenings. This meant pizza and movies!

Finally, my husband started to laugh again and come back to life. But, every now and again, he just needs time to think things through.

I still worry about him today because he will still walk away from us, occasionally, and enter into that other world again, where no one else is allowed. He just doesn't stay there as long as he used to anymore.

For twenty-two years, Syd worked with these thoughts and feelings. Finally, he retired from the police force in July 2008, after taking annual leave. Now he is starting to live! Although he had written a couple of short articles for police officers about the shooting incident, the best therapy for him has been writing this book.

Syd will never be the same person I married. I married one Syd but ended up living with another with two very distinct personalities. One person lives strictly by the rules and is very impatient, quiet, reserved and contemplative—a deep thinker. The other person is happy go lucky and fun loving, spontaneous and excitingly unpredictable. I have learned to live with both of them as and when they appear and I love them both.

Endnote

1. This letter was previously published and the writer has given permission for it to be reprinted here with some editing for style and to remove names.

Letting Go

I once heard an elder from the Mohawk Nation describe how there is a circle of creation that takes you from the creator to earth and then, when your time on earth is done, as decided by the creator, let go and allow the circle to return you to the creator. This is good advice.

The same can be said of your problems. Let them go. Don't ignore them but don't carry them around until the carrying itself becomes the problem.

Tanzan (18??-1892) was a Buddhist monk and professor of philosophy at the Japanese Imperial University (now the University of Tokyo) during the Meiji Period. Considered a Zen master, he figures in several well-known koans. He was also well known for his disregard of many of the precepts of everyday Buddhism such as the dietary laws.

The following is one of his most famous stories called *The Muddy Road*:

> Tanzan and Ekido were once traveling together down a muddy road. A heavy rain was falling. As they came around the bend, they met a lovely girl in a silk kimono and sash unable to cross at an intersection.
>
> "Come on, girl," said Tanzan at once. Lifting her in his arms, he carried her over the mud.
>
> Ekido did not speak until that night when they reached a lodging temple. Then he could no longer restrain himself. "We

monks don't go near females," he told Tanzan, "especially not young and lovely ones. It is dangerous. Why did you do that?"

"I left the girl there," said Tanzan. "Are you still carrying her?" (Excerpt from *Wikipedia*, the free encyclopedia.)

Letting go of a problem is always difficult and sometimes you should not try to do it alone. All members should remember this as they work their way through stressful situations.

No matter how angry or discouraged you are, you cannot stop the sun from rising or the stars from shining, so don't forget to appreciate and look forward to each day or night as if it is a gift, as the creator has indeed made it so.

There is a quote from Eleanor Powell, an American actress and dancer, that goes: "What we are is God's gift to us. What we become is our gift to God."

Eventually, I came to realize that the guy who was hurting me the most was me. I stayed angry far too long. Once I realized that I was harder on myself than anyone else was, I was more capable of facing the challenges of trying to get along with others and letting go.

Twenty-Five Years Later

Twenty-five years later, I still suffer from the effects of PTSD. I still have moments where I have difficulty controlling my emotions, sometimes getting overly emotional or becoming very frustrated or angry without apparent reason. The difference now is that I know what the symptoms are and have made them a part of who I am and a part of my life. I accept them, react to them appropriately and move on. I understand now where these feelings come from; I just don't know when they will appear or with what intensity.

Sometimes, when these symptoms occur, I just have to walk away from people and take some time for myself to think about things long past or just take a moment to reflect on the paths not taken. Once this is done, I move on. I have come to accept that these feelings will return periodically.

The other symptoms that have never left me and that have hit me the hardest are the constant second guessing and the lack of confidence. For those who worked with me in policing over the years, I projected considerable confidence at work and in the police environment. But the truth is that I struggled with self-confidence almost every day.

To this day, I still suffer from constant second guessing my decisions and constantly worry about the consequences of decisions I take, sometimes, to the point of obsessiveness. Those around me bear the burden of listening to me mull over every decision I make.

One other symptom that still lingers, but not as severely, is the inability to sleep well. For the longest time, I would wake up at a certain hour every night, unable to go back to sleep. I will go months without it happening and, then, without warning, it starts over again. Now, I get up, sit quietly in my favourite chair in the living room and simply think things through or read a good book. Eventually, I fall asleep in the chair.

I have learned to accept these recurring symptoms and not to fight them. By accepting them, they have become a part of who I am and not something I try to hide. This is who I am now, living with PTSD. And crucial to my well-being throughout these episodes is my relationship with my family, friends and the members of my peer support group.

Peer Support History in Ottawa

The Robin's Blue Circle was formed in Ottawa in 1988, when police officers got together, under the guidance of Dr. Pierre Turgeon, a professor at the University of Ottawa, to help each other through the effects of post-shooting trauma as a result of work-related incidents. Dr. Turgeon's constant advice to us was that "our reactions were normal reactions to abnormal situations." It was important to grasp that message first and foremost. The support group was named after Robin Easey, a Nepean police officer with 21 Division, who survived a near-fatal bullet wound to the back of the head during a botched robbery. He is one of the founding fathers of the peer support team.

The original members included four officers from the Ottawa Police Service, two from the Nepean Police Service and one from the Royal Canadian Mounted Police (RCMP). Four of the members had been shot and had survived; three members had fatally shot a suspect. The members of the group saw the healing process as a circle back to their normal routine after having been involved in situations that had disrupted their daily life, thus, the name Robin's Blue Circle. Since 1988, the circle has grown to include members from across Canada. They understood each other as no one had ever understood them since their events.

Peer support members believe that officers involved in fatal or near-fatal incidents should not try to forget or pretend that the event never occurred. They also believe that officers should not stay alone, except when time alone is needed to gather their thoughts. What they need to know and learn is that the event is now part of their life and part of their character; they need to move on with their life and the knowledge of the incident entrenched within their life and who they are now. The process of accepting this is shown in the blue circle as seen in illustration A.

Illustration A: The Blue Circle

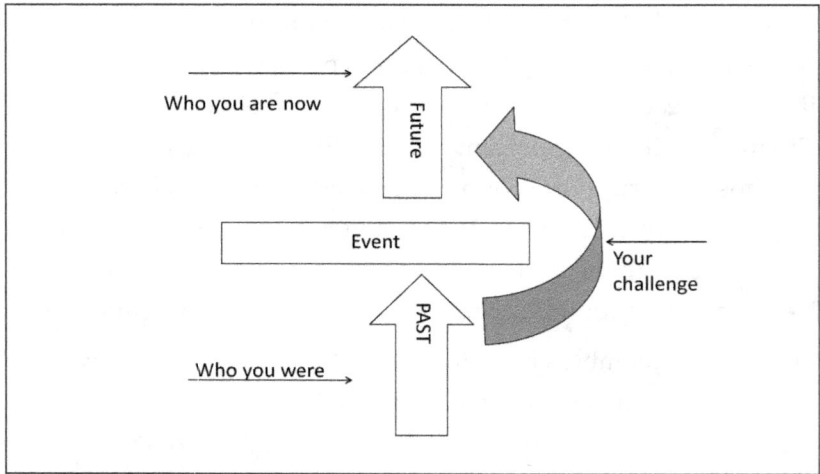

The diagram shows how officers move in a circle from who they were to who they become.

One of the keys to our success has been the fact that, as a group of police officers, we have come to understand our pain. Over the years, I have identified four rules to guide our members, five stages in the healing process and recognized the eight most common symptoms of posttraumatic stress disorder (PTSD). These help us to understand and work through PTSD.

The Four Rules

The following four rules have been established to guide the peer support group.

1. We claim no qualifications other than to have experienced personally the difficulty an officer has in getting reconnected to life after the trauma that we have lived with. Members are a shoulder to lean on, an ear to listen and a voice during the darkest moments that will whisper, "We know what you are saying." We deal strictly within the realm of only what we have personally experienced. For members, honesty and trust are crucial.

2. We answer only to the member we are supporting.

3. We advise that, first and foremost, the subject officer should seek professional help at least once to ensure that they are given all the help they need.

4. We assure each member that confidentiality is paramount.

The Five Stages

The following five stages have been identified as part of the healing process to help a member deal with PTSD.

1. That we share our experiences. Each member is encouraged to share their emotions and feelings as a result of the event and how these have impacted the member at the time the event occurred and since then. (This does not mean that the member officer reveals the details of the event to the detriment of their legal rights. Those details are between the member, their legal advisor and the investigators.)

2. That we understand and acknowledge the importance of seeking support from a professional. Each member is asked to consider this option at least once.

3. That we discuss and recognize how our families are affected by the member's trauma as well. Each member needs to consider the consequences of the event on their loved ones.

4. That we understand, from every traumatic experience, there is a silver lining. Each member is encouraged to look for some positive outcome from the traumatic event.

5. That peace can be found in reconnecting or staying connected with the spiritual side of one's life. Each member has an opportunity to discuss their spirituality in whatever form that may take, as long as it works for the member. Each member needs to understand that no matter how difficult things have become at the moment, life goes on regardless of our inner turmoil.

The Eight Most Common Symptoms

The following eight most common symptoms have been identified to help forewarn the officer as the most probable symptoms they may face. (*See* the chapter titled "Moving Forward" for more details.) Briefly these symptoms are:

1. Denial. That the member recognizes that they have a problem rather than denying it.

2. Loneliness. That the member officer feels alone in dealing with their experience.

3. Second guessing and loss of self-confidence. That the officer begins to second guess decisions and has lost confidence in their ability to take a decision.

4. Loss of emotional control. That members will experience emotional swings immediately after an incident.

5. Loss of sleep and appetite control. That member officers notice disruptions in their sleep patterns or in their eating habits.

6. Obsessing over public opinion. That some police officers will become more aware of or concerned with what the public thinks or with what is reported.

7. Fear of loss of peer support. That members need to accept support when and where it is offered and fear that they will lose the support of their family and others as a consequence of their actions.

8. Fear of not protecting family and loved ones. That members realize their need to protect their family is natural but they need to share their feelings as well.

Peer Supporters

Peer supporters in the Blue Circle are officers who have survived the ultimate decision in police work, that is, to discharge their weapon during a particular situation with a fatal or near-fatal consequence to another human. We make no pretence to advise or counsel fellow officers beyond what we have experienced ourselves. We listen, provide support and are a shoulder to lean on. If we see trauma setting in, we direct the officer to the proper professional medical attention and support them when they admit they need help.

We do not interfere with the investigative process but concentrate on the officer's emotional well-being, so that the investigative process can be completed.

After starting Robin's Blue Circle, several of the officers assisted in supporting fellow officers often in circumstances that were detrimental to their own careers. Although not accepted initially as a resource by senior administration, members would often be asked by street-level supervisors to respond to calls where officers were involved in shooting incidents. Sometimes, all we had to do at first was show up at work and stand in the hallway, so that a subject officer could see us standing there. Just by doing that, the officer knew that they were not alone. As members of the circle, we have vowed never to leave an officer on their own as they deal with the consequences of a shooting incident.

In one incident, the chief of police asked me how he could help. I suggested that he meet me at the station. We stood in the hallway and simply nodded to the suspect officer to let him know we cared about him. Many times, this was all that was necessary to help the officer on the road to a quick recovery. It didn't eliminate the consequences that they would face. But they saw that there was support.

My Personal Involvement

As one officer stated, when he first joined Robin's Blue Circle, "You're a wonderful bunch of people, but the price to join your club is way too expensive!" I can attest to this as I personally have responded to over forty calls to help police officers after their incidents, over a period of twelve years. In the thirteenth year, I realized I could no longer continue to pay the fees. Every time I stepped forward to help someone who had fallen, I had to get back on my knees as well. They needed to see me down there with them, so that we could get back up together. And, getting back up was becoming harder to do every time.

In 2008, I retired from the police service. In my exit interview with the chief, I explained how I had come to work every day for twenty-two years in a state of fear. I feared that, on any given day, someone out there would again force me to make a decision that might have fatal or near-fatal consequences. I was not sure that I wanted to go through that whole process again. The chief was taken aback by my revelation and stated that there had not been any sense of this in any of my work. I was a professional and kept my inner turmoil to myself.

Subsequent to my retirement, I was asked if I would help some Aboriginal and Inuit police officers, who were in need of direction, support and advice. I have developed a three-day workshop to help them form their own peer support networks, which have been well received by the Aboriginal and Inuit policing communities in Quebec and Labrador. I have been holding these workshops since my departure from policing in 2008. (*See* appendixes 1, 2 and 3 for generic agendas.)

After Word

Due to the initial support of the Ottawa-Carleton Regional Police Services Chiefs Thomas G. Flanagan and Brian J. Ford, along with Deputy Chief Don Lyon and John Petersen, president of the Ottawa-Carleton Regional Police Association, the Ottawa Police Service has within its structure a highly skilled and responsive crisis intervention team.

Through the training provided by the crisis intervention workers, there are now over sixty trained crisis intervention support members. They were drawn from all ranks and civilian members of the Ottawa Police Service. Aside from the trauma team, there are also thirty-five members of a post-shooting trauma team. This self-help group, called Robin's Blue Circle, comprises officers who have survived shootings either as victims or as shootists. Together, they have developed a strong bond with many other officers throughout Canada in their desire to see that officers, who have done their duty, are respected for having done so.

This struggle to provide support has not been without some personal setbacks for its members. However, on the whole, they have seen major changes in how police services, workers' compensation and fellow officers—through crisis intervention— now deal with these living heroes.

This is quite a change from a time when officers were once thought to be able "to get over it" by having a meeting with Jack Daniels. As can be seen, everyone benefits from officers being treated for posttraumatic reactions immediately following traumatic incidents.

Appendix 1

Three-Day Workshop:
Introduction to Peer Support

Objective

To develop a peer support network managed by members of an organization. This workshop is geared toward members who need peer support and to those who want to be peer support workers.

This peer support network will assist its members in addressing posttraumatic stress symptoms in relation to work-related events. Whether they are dealing with an incident-specific event or a long-term accumulation of events, members will learn to address posttraumatic symptoms in a safe environment, surrounded by peer supporters, family, crisis intervention specialists and medical practitioners, if available. The overarching objective of the peer support network, supported by management and monitored by crisis intervention or medical professionals, is to enable their members to become fully capable of returning to work as soon as possible.

Program Overview

The program consists of three days of comprehensive and interactive work with members of the organization, who have experienced traumatic events either specific to one incident or as an accumulation of events over time. Members will review the four rules that guide a peer support network, the five stages one goes through in the healing process, and the eight most common symptoms experienced by members suffering from posttraumatic stress disorder. The workshop facilitator will lead everyone through each step by sharing his/her own personal experiences.

Caveat: In order to deliver maximum value and results, each peer supporter must have experienced their own specific traumatic event, or a series of traumatic events, which has led them to take part in this workshop. Because it is extremely important to establish trust among peers, peer members must be credible and have personal experience with trauma.

NOTE: The purpose of the workshop is to assist officers and emergency personnel in creating a peer support structure that helps healing to happen. It is not the intent in forming this group to eliminate or replace the valuable use and existence of certified peer/family support crisis incident stress management personnel, or mental or medical health practitioners. If the organization has a certified crisis intervention worker or mental or medical health practitioners on staff, who could attend the three-day workshop with members, they would be most welcome in establishing the important relationship between peer support members and certified crisis intervention workers or mental or medical health practitioners.

Agendas

Day One: Welcome to Members

1. Welcome and Introductions
2. The Story behind Peer Support Networks
3. My Story: What Did You Hear?
4. Participants Tell Their Stories
5. Why We Are at This Workshop

Day Two: Members (optional for members' spouses/partners to attend this day)

6. Leading Each Other through the Process

7. Reflecting and Sharing about Family

8. The Importance of a Silver Lining

9. Members' Awareness

Day Three: Members (optional for members' spouses/partners)

10. Continuing Peer Support

11. Confidentiality

12. Healing Processes

13. Next Steps

Workshops usually run from 0900 to 1700 hours, with a one-hour lunch break and two fifteen-minute breaks.

Day One

1. Welcome and Introductions. The facilitator, who is both an experienced peer support member and facilitator, will lead the welcome by ensuring that each member understands that they are in a safe, supportive, respectful and bias-free environment, where each member will feel comfortable and be encouraged to share their feelings without judgement. The facilitator will introduce his/herself, touching briefly on their background and their reasons for being part of the peer support network. They will then encourage each participant to do the same. There are no time limits imposed on participants to accomplish the introduction, as this is the first step for members to realize how safe the environment is for them.

    The facilitator will then introduce participants to the four rules that guide peer support, the five stages in the healing process and the eight most commonly experienced symptoms.

2. The Story behind Peer Support Networks. The facilitator will provide an example of a peer support network, whichever example he/she is most familiar with, to help members see what the structure can look like.

One example of such a network is the Ottawa Police Service group, known as Robin's Blue Circle. Named after Robin Easey, a then Nepean police officer, who survived a near-fatal bullet wound to the back of the head during a botched robbery, Robin is one of the founding members of the peer support team.

This network was formed in 1988; it was one of the first post-shooting trauma peer support networks established in Canada. It was the foundation on which many other police services studied and established their own programs. Its founding members were from the Ottawa Police Service (4), the Nepean Police Service (2) and the RCMP (1). Four members had been shot and survived, and three members had fatally shot suspects.

3. My Story: What Did You Hear? The facilitator shares his/her story to help establish a safe environment in the workshop and uses his/her own event to describe how they came to need and appreciate peer support. The details of the event are not as important as the reaction and feelings described by the member as a result of being involved in an event, or an accumulation of events, that has affected them.

Each participant is then asked to sum up what they heard about how a member was affected by the event or events. This assists peer supporters in learning to share and listen.

4. Participants Tell Their Stories. Each member is then encouraged and supported in telling their own story and their reaction to the event, or accumulated events, which has brought them to

participate in this workshop. Each participant is then asked to sum up what they heard about how each member was affected by the event or events.

5. Why We Are at This Workshop. Not everyone wants to be a peer support worker. It takes hard work and courage to be one. The facilitator may describe how she/he has to relive their own traumatic experience each time they work with an officer or member who needs their support. This can be very difficult for some members, especially those who want to move on as quickly as possible. Many participants may simply want to know that there is a group available, which they can talk to if they need to. Everyone discusses why they are involved and what they hope to accomplish by participating in the workshop. This helps to establish who the potential peer support workers are.

Day Two

Family structure and support are discussed. Some participants may wish to invite their spouses to take part in the workshop and are welcome to do so.

Any issues remaining from day one should be completed before beginning the day-two agenda.

6. Leading Each Other through the Process. Members discuss what they think will help them through their situations. By sharing, they learn that not everyone needs the same type of support.

7. Reflecting and Sharing about Family. Members share the effects their event, or series of events, has had on their family. Family members can also share how they were affected by the events, or series of events, over time and how they thought they had to cope. Members will also learn how their families have been affected.

8. The Importance of a Silver Lining. Members discuss what may have been the silver lining in the traumatic event that occurred in their lives. For many, the outcome may be increased closeness to their family. Others have found that their experience has given them wisdom, an awareness of how life can turn on a moment's notice and how to prepare for this in the future. Others may not have had the support of the organization or their peers, which they needed at the time, and the event has created a personal challenge from which they have survived, despite the lack of support. They may believe that they are stronger personally as a result.

9. Members' Awareness. For those who cannot connect with family or find a silver lining, they are recognized as members who need peer support after the workshop is completed. Since these members may have shared what they need the most (see #6), peer support members should be aware of how they can help the most and immediately.

Day Three

Some participants may wish to invite their spouses to take part in day three and are welcome to do so.

Any issues remaining from day two should be completed before beginning the day-three agenda.

10. Continuing Peer Support. Members discuss the infrastructure required from within their organization to help support their newly established peer-support network.

11. Confidentiality. Issues surrounding confidentiality are discussed and agreements are reached with regard to respecting each other's privacy and rights.

12. Healing Processes. Members discuss the availability and participation of professional support for the peer network such as the presence and involvement of a certified crisis intervention worker, a psychiatrist or psychologist or a family physician.

13. Next Steps. Participants are asked for any final comments.

Appendix 2

Two-Day Workshop for a Newly Established Peer Support Network

Objective

To support a newly established peer support network managed by members of an organization. This workshop is for participants who want to become peer supporters.

This peer support network will assist its members in addressing posttraumatic stress symptoms in relation to work-related events. Whether they are dealing with an incident-specific event or a long-term accumulation of events, participants will learn to support their peers in addressing posttraumatic symptoms in a safe environment, surrounded by peer supporters, family, crisis intervention specialists and medical practitioners, if available. The overarching objective of the peer support network, supported by management and monitored by crisis intervention or medical professionals, is to enable their members to become fully capable of returning to work as soon as possible.

Program Overview

The program consists of two days of comprehensive and interactive work with members of the organization, who have experienced traumatic events, either specific to one incident or as an accumulation of events over time, and who want to manage their own network as peer supporters. Members will review the four rules that guide a peer support network, the five stages one goes through in the healing process, and the eight most common symptoms experienced by members suffering from posttraumatic stress disorder. The workshop facilitator will lead everyone through each step by sharing his/her own personal experiences.

Caveat: In order to deliver maximum value and results, each member must have experienced their own specific traumatic event, or a series of traumatic events, which has led them to take part in this workshop. Because it is extremely important to establish trust among peers, members must be credible and have personal experience with trauma.

NOTE: The purpose of the workshop is to assist officers and emergency personnel in creating a peer support structure that helps healing to happen. It is not the intent in forming this group to eliminate or replace the valuable use and existence of certified peer/family support crisis incident stress management personnel, or mental or medical health practitioners. If the organization has a certified crisis intervention worker or mental or medical health practitioners on staff, who could attend the two-day workshop with members, they would be most welcome in establishing the important relationship between peer support members and certified crisis intervention workers or mental or medical health practitioners.

Agendas

Day One: Welcome to Members

1. Welcome and Introductions
2. The Story behind Peer Support Networks
3. My Story: What Did You Hear?
4. Participants Tell Their Stories
5. Why We Are at This Workshop

Day Two: Members (optional for members' spouses/partners to attend)

6. Leading Each Other through the Process

7. Reflecting and Sharing about Family

8. The Importance of a Silver Lining

9. Members' Awareness, Confidentiality and Healing Processes

10. Next Steps

Workshops usually run from 0900 hours to 1700 hours, with a one-hour lunch break and two fifteen-minute breaks.

Day One

1. Welcome and Introductions. The facilitator, who is both an experienced peer support member and facilitator, will lead the welcome by ensuring that each member understands that they are in a safe, supportive, respectful and bias-free environment, where each member will feel comfortable and be encouraged to share their feelings without judgement. The facilitator will introduce his/herself, touching briefly on their background and their reasons for being part of a peer support network. They will then encourage each participant to do the same. There are no time limits imposed on participants to accomplish this introduction, as this is the first step for them to realize how safe the environment is for them.

   The facilitator will then introduce the four rules that guide a peer support network, the five stages in the healing process and the eight most commonly experienced symptoms.

2. The Story behind Peer Support Networks. The facilitator will provide an example of a peer support network, whichever example he/she is most familiar with, to help members see what the structure can look like.

   One example of such a network is the Ottawa Police Service group, known as Robin's Blue Circle. Named after Robin Easey, a then Nepean police officer, who survived a near fatal-bullet wound to the back of the head during a botched robbery, Robin is one of the founding members of the peer support team.

This network was formed in 1988; it was one of the first post-shooting trauma peer support networks established in Canada. It was the foundation on which many other police services studied and established their own programs. Its founding members were from the Ottawa Police Service (4), the Nepean Police Service (2) and the RCMP (1). Four members had been shot and survived, and three members had fatally shot suspects.

3. My Story: What Did You Hear? The facilitator shares his/her story to help establish a safe environment in the workshop and uses his/her own event to describe how they came to need and appreciate peer support. The details of the event are not as important as the reaction and feelings described by the member as a result of being involved in an event, or an accumulation of events, that has affected them.

   Each participant is then asked to sum up what they heard about how the member was affected by the event or events. This assists peer supporters in learning to share and listen.

4. Participants Tell Their Stories. Each member is then encouraged and supported in telling their own story and their reaction to the event, or accumulated events, which has brought them to participate in this workshop. Each participant is then asked to sum up what they heard about how each member was affected by the event or events.

5. Why We Are at This Workshop. Since everyone participating wants to be a peer supporter, the facilitator needs to explain that it

will take hard work and courage, because a peer support worker has to relive their own traumatic experience each time they work with an officer or member who needs their support. This can be very difficult for some members.

Each participant discusses why they are involved and what they hope to accomplish by participating in the workshop. This helps to establish the foundation in becoming a peer supporter.

Day Two

Family structure and support are discussed. Some participants may wish to invite their spouses to take part in the workshop and are welcome to do so. However, as peer supporters they are encouraged to form a spousal support network as well.

Any issues remaining from day one should be completed before beginning the day-two agenda.

6. Leading Each Other through a Process. Participants discuss what they think will help them through their situations. By sharing, they learn that not everyone needs the same type of support.

7. Reflecting and Sharing about Family. Participants share the effects their event, or series of events, has had on their family. Family members can also share how they were affected by the event, or series of events, over time and how they thought they had to cope. Members will also learn how their families have been affected.

8. The Importance of a Silver Lining. Members discuss what may have been the silver lining in the traumatic event that occurred in their lives. For many, the outcome may be closeness with their family. Others have found that their experience has given them wisdom, an awareness of how life can turn on a moment's notice and how to prepare for this in the future. Others may not have

had the support of the organization or their peers, which they needed at the time, and the event has created a personal challenge from which they have survived, despite the lack of support. They may believe they are stronger personally as a result.

9. Members' Awareness, Confidentiality and Healing Processes. Participants have shared what they need the most (see #6), so members are already aware of how they can most immediately and best help their peers.

Issues surrounding confidentiality are discussed and agreements are reached with regard to respecting each other's privacy and rights.

Members discuss the availability and participation of professional support for the peer network such as the presence and involvement of a certified crisis intervention worker, a psychiatrist or psychologist or family physician.

10. Next Steps. Participants are asked for any final comments and plan the launch of the first peer support network meeting.

Appendix 3

Peer Support Meeting
Where a Network Exists

Objective

For peers to support members of an organization who have been involved in an event, or series of events, that has resulted in the need for peer support.

This peer support network meeting will assist its members in addressing posttraumatic stress symptoms in relation to work-related events. Whether they are dealing with an incident-specific event or a long-term accumulation of events, the meeting will introduce the members to their peer supporters and they will learn how to assist members in addressing their posttraumatic symptoms in a safe environment, surrounded by peer supporters, family, crisis intervention specialists and medical practitioners, if available. The overarching objective of the peer support network, supported by management and monitored by crisis intervention or medical professionals, is to enable their members to become fully capable of returning to work as soon as possible.

Meeting Overview

The meeting consists of comprehensive and interactive work with members of the organization, who have experienced traumatic events, either specific to one incident or as an accumulation of events over time, and who want support from their own peers. They will be advised that they are participating in a safe, supportive, respectful and bias-free environment, where the members will feel comfortable and be encouraged to share their feelings without any judgement.

They will review the four rules that guide the peer support network, the five stages one goes through in the healing process, and the eight most common symptoms experienced by members suffering from posttraumatic stress disorder. The meeting facilitator will lead members through each step.

Caveat: In order to deliver maximum value and results, each peer supporter must have experienced their own specific traumatic event, or a series of traumatic events, which has led them to take part in this meeting as a peer supporter. Because it is extremely important to establish trust among peers, peer supporters must be credible and have personal experience with trauma

NOTE: The purpose of the meeting is to assist officers and emergency personnel in addressing the trauma associated with an event or series of events that are work related. It is not the intent in forming this group to eliminate or replace the valuable use and existence of certified peer/family support crisis incident stress management personnel, or mental or medical health practitioners. If the organization has a certified crisis intervention worker or mental or medical health practitioners on staff, who could attend the meeting with the members, they would be most welcome in establishing the important relationship between peer support members and certified crisis intervention workers or mental or medical health practitioners.

Agenda

1. Welcome and Introduction of Peer Supporters to New Members

2. Recap of Each Peer Supporter's Story for New Members

3. Introduction of the Four Rules That Guide the Peer Support Network and the Five Stages One Goes through in the Healing Process

4. New Members Share Their Story and Identify Their Needs and Issues

5. Sharing the Eight Symptoms Most Commonly Experienced

6. Identifying and Addressing New Members' Needs

7. Commitment to Assist until the Next Required Meeting

Agenda Steps

1. Welcome and Introduction of Peer Supporters to New Members. The facilitator, who is both an experienced peer support member and facilitator, will lead the welcome by ensuring that each new member understands that they are in a safe, supportive, respectful and bias-free environment, where each member will feel comfortable and encouraged to share their feelings without judgement.

2. Recap of Each Peer Supporter's Story for New Members. The meeting facilitator will introduce her/himself, touching briefly on their background and reasons for being a part of the peer support network. They will then ask each peer supporter attending to do the same. Generally, these recaps are presented in summary format and simply as an introduction of peer supporters to new members.

3. Introduction of the Four Rules That Guide the Peer Support Network and the Five Stages One Goes through in the Healing Process. The facilitator discusses the four rules to reassure new members that there is a formal structure to the meeting and the group's existence. The facilitator also points out that there are five stages that they will be supported through to help in the healing process.

4. New Members Share Their Story and Identify Their Needs and Issues. New members are the encouraged to share what brought them to the point of needing peer support and why they need it, so that peer supporters can prepare plans to support the members.

5. Sharing the Eight Symptoms Most Commonly Experienced. Peer supporters share with the new members the eight most common

symptoms experienced by those suffering from posttraumatic stress disorder. Some peer supporters may also share other additional symptoms that they have suffered. This helps new members to normalize their situation.

6. Identifying and Addressing New Members' Needs. Once symptoms are described, new members may acknowledge some of these as part of their concerns. They may identify others as well. Peer supporters can now start to plan the process of supporting the new members.

7. Commitment to Assist until the Next Required Meeting. Peer supporters and new members agree to work together to support each other until the next meeting. Meetings can also be held one on one if agreed to, or another meeting may include more peer supporters as required. Meetings can be held as often as needed.

About the Author

Syd Gravel was a police officer with the Ottawa Police Service for over thirty years. During his first twenty years, he was a frontline officer in a variety of patrol functions. For the last ten years, he was involved in training and recruitment. He retired from the Ottawa Police Service with the rank of staff sergeant.

Syd is one of the founding members of the Robin's Blue Circle, a post-shooting trauma team that assists officers in working their way through the trauma of death or near-death, work-related incidents. Over a period of twelve years, he has personally assisted over forty officers to survive near-death incidents.

His work has been recognized and his projects have received the following: the 2006 and 2008 Top Ten International Innovation in Diversity Awards, from *Profiles in Diversity Journal*, Cleveland, Ohio; and the 2007 International Chiefs of Police Civil Rights Award, New Orleans, Louisiana.

In January 1999, he received the police Exemplary Service Medal from the governor general of Canada, His Excellency the Right Honourable Romeo LeBlanc. In January 2007, he was inducted as a Member of the Order of Merit (MOM) in Policing and invested by the then Governor General, Her Excellency the Right Honourable Michaëlle Jean.

Syd was also a keynote speaker at the First Canadian Forum on Traumatic Stress Conference, held in Toronto, presenting on "Surviving Post-Shooting Trauma," and a guest lecturer for

Correctional Services Canada, in Kingston, lecturing on "Wellness and Traumatic Stress." He was also the keynote speaker at the International Conference on Conservation Officers, held in Ottawa, and titled, "Stress Management and Its Realities."

Since 2008, Syd and his Montreal workshop partner, retired Corporal Merritt Eaton, have facilitated at annual workshops at the Dialogue for Life Conferences in Montreal. These are attended by First Nations' police officers and organized by the First Nations and Inuit Suicide Prevention Association of Quebec and Labrador. These officers began to form their own First Nations Police Officers' Peace Circle, modeled after the Ottawa Police Services' Robin's Blue Circle. The First Nations police officers, who attended, were from the Montagnais, Atikamekw and Cree Nations. This work is ongoing.

Syd Gravel can be reached at www.56secondsbook.com or www.56secondsbook.ca.

I started my policing career in 1988 and came to know Syd Gravel in March 1995. I was severely injured while attempting to apprehend four suspects who had committed an armed bank robbery. I was shot through the right shoulder—the bullet traveled to my upper body around the ribs and ended up between my shoulder blade and spine. My shoulder had severe nerve damage and my arm was partially paralyzed for about eighteen months. Doctors and medical experts believed I would not recover from my injuries or return to work.

As challenging as the physical injuries were—and the excruciating pain—that was nothing compared to the difficulty in dealing with the emotional and psychological trauma in my darkest hours, days, months and years that followed.

Peer support was a key factor in my physical and mental recovery from this traumatic event. The most significant thing about peer support is that you are dealing with people who have lived through similar experiences. They can provide a deeper level of understanding—often without even saying a word—an understanding that no health care professional can provide or comprehend.

The pioneering work done by Syd and the other founding members of Robin's Blue Circle has no doubt paved the way for other critical incident support resources for police officers.

Now in my twenty-fourth year of policing, I am forever indebted to my wife, my family and members of Robin's Blue Circle for giving me the support needed to enable my return to active duty. I offer my heartfelt gratitude to Syd for his personal commitment and dedication to helping others.

– J.P. A POLICE SHOOTING SURVIVOR WITH 24 YEARS IN POLICING AND STILL COUNTING